TOXIC PRODUCTS AND BAD BUSINESS FROM COMMUNIST CHINA

**MUST-READ BOOK FOR ANYONE
DOING BUSINESS WITH
COMMUNIST CHINA
OR TRAVELING THERE**

TOXIC PRODUCTS

HACKING

THEFT

ANDREJS "ANDY" BAUMHAMMERS DDS MS

PROGRESSIVE PROJECTS LLC

LIMITATIONS OF LIABILITY /
DISCLAIMER OF WARRANTY

The author and publisher have used their best
efforts to provide accurate information.
However, in a time of rapid change, it is difficult
to ensure that all the information provided is
accurate and up-to-date. The author and
publisher are not engaged in rendering business,
health or medical services. Therefore, you
should consult with a qualified professional
where appropriate. Accordingly, the author and
publisher make no representations or warranties
for any inaccuracies or omissions, and
specifically disclaim any liability, loss, whether
personal, financial or otherwise which is
incurred as a consequence, directly or indirectly,
from the use and/or application of any contents
of this book.

ISBN: 9781705506813

DEDICATION

This book is dedicated to Democracy. With all its problems, it is a far better government system for the people of a country than Communism, Nazism, Fascism or Dictatorship. The author himself has lived under Communism, Nazism and Democracy.

CONTENTS

INTRODUCTION

One may ask, "Why write a book on Chinese toxic products and Chinese shady business practices?" Let us first establish what China is. China is officially called the People's Republic of China. However, I like to call it Communist China, which is what it really is. China has a very large population of 1.379 billion people as of September 2018. Mao Zedong proclaimed a People's Republic of China on October 1, 1949. For a long time, China was a primarily agrarian society. Only since the ascendancy of leader Deng Xiaoping in 1978[1] did it start to truly industrialize, becoming the second largest economy in the world, behind the United States.

However, improvement in the economy did not improve individual freedoms such as freedom of speech, freedom of travel, and respect for civil and human rights.[2] That has yet to come, but who knows how far in the future that will be. There is even strict censorship of the internet and social media in China. Those who dare to write or speak unfavorably of communist China are retaliated against, ostracized, and often go to jail.[3]

Furthermore, in the mad rush to modernize and industrialize China and improve its economy, few measures were taken to protect the public from defective and toxic products. The purpose of this book is to document these harmful products and practices. Since the United States is the largest trading partner of communist China, it has also borne the brunt of some of these harmful and toxic products.

To the extent that it is possible, I have tried to give credit in this book to the sources of my information, such as news reports, newspaper articles, and information that I located on the internet. I have spent years collecting material on the topics covered in this book and all this material now is in one place. This book should be read by everybody buying Chinese manufactured products in the West, everybody doing business with China, and everybody who plans to travel to China for any significant length of time. My goal has been to keep each chapter direct and concise so that readers can access this essential information quickly and easily. The book by Peter Navarro and Greg Autry titled Death by China covers similar material, and is a good follow-up read for anyone seeking more in-depth information.[4]

CHAPTER 1
DEADLY CARFENTANIL SHIPMENT PROBLEMS FROM CHINA

Carfentanil is closely tied in with the opioid epidemic. In the United States, government officials at all levels—city, state, and federal—agree there is an opioid epidemic across the country, from rural small towns to large cities to affluent suburbs. How did this happen? US pharmaceutical companies, such as Purdue Pharma, pushed the sales of highly addictive opioids like OxyContin even though they knew that the drugs were addictive.[1] Once patients suffering from pain got addicted, they could no longer afford the high cost of the legal opioid pills or could not get refills, and turned to cheaper street drugs, such as heroin. However, for several years drug dealers have cut heroin with Chinese carfentanil, whose dose is very unpredictable, resulting in overdoses and thousands of deaths.[2]

What is carfentanil, and why should it matter to us?

Carfentanil is the most powerful synthetic narcotic on earth and it is finding its way into USA from China by US Postal Service or through Mexico. Drug dealers are using it to extend the supply of heroin by mixing it with heroin.[2] The Associated Press reported that 12 Chinese companies offered to export carfentanil for a few thousand dollars a kilo, "no questions asked." But the substance is so strong—5000 times stronger than heroin—and so toxic that many consider it a chemical weapon. According to the same AP report, "an amount smaller than a poppy seed can kill a person," making it impossible for those who wish to use it as a recreational drug to determine the appropriate dose that will provide a high without endangering their lives.[3] According to the National Center for Biotechnology Information, "It is marketed under the trade name Wildnil as a general anaesthetic agent for large animals. Carfentanil is intended for large-animal use only as its extreme potency makes it inappropriate for use in humans."[4] Fortunately, in 2017 China added this deadly tranquilizer and three other related synthetic opioids to its list of controlled substances, according to China's National Narcotics Control Commission.[5]

Although all opioids, legal and illegal, are subject to abuse, carfentanil is especially pernicious because first responders (such as police and EMS personnel) may have difficulty providing countermeasures to people who have overdosed on this powerful drug. The treatment drug Naloxone, which reverses the effects of opioids, may need to be administered several times.[6] First responders also have to be careful not to become accidentally contaminated with carfentanil, since they too could become sick or overdose. Symptoms of exposure include disorientation, breathing problems, sedation, and shrunken pupils, and occur within minutes.[6]

Senator Rob Portman (R-OH) has co-sponsored a bill called the Synthetics Trafficking and Overdose Prevention, or STOP, act. He says that the illicit sellers in China avoid private carriers like FedEx or UPS because they require tracking information from the sender, but with the US mail system that is not required. Chinese distributors send packages through the US Mail system without that information. The new law would require the U.S. Postal Service to track senders the same way as private shippers do.[7]

CHAPTER 2
TOXIC CHINESE DRYWALL

A big part of what is called the "American dream" is owning a home. It is a monumental problem when one part of that home has toxic material in it—as is the case with some drywall produced in China. Drywall, a basic building material in the construction of houses, is made of a large sheets of plaster covered with thick paper.[1] It was invented in 1916 and has been used since the 1940s as an essential part of house construction, and is typically used to create the interior walls of the home.[2]

In the 2000s there was a relative shortage of drywall due to natural disasters such as hurricanes Katrina and Rita.[3] Therefore, to keep up with the demand for drywall, the United States began importing it from China, mostly from 2004 to 2008.[3] Soon after, reports that there was corrosion in houses that were constructed using Chinese drywall began to surface[4]. Pyrite—a mineral which is part of the plaster in drywall--underwent oxidation, releasing sulfur gases. It is these sulfur gases that cause the corrosion of other elements within homes, especially of copper.[5]

There are two signs that could suggest that your home may be contaminated with toxic drywall and three steps you can take to check on it. If your home has a strong odor reminiscent of rotten eggs, or if your copper wiring looks dark and corroded, this may signal that you have toxic drywall. Silverware and silver jewelry may also become tarnished due to the sulfur gases. It may take months of exposure for this corrosion to occur.

If you are concerned that you may have toxic drywall in your home, check for a manufacturer's label on the back of the drywall to identify those manufacturers who are linked to using hazardous materials. These labels can be usually be found in the attic behind the insulation. Some of the large manufacturers were Knauf Plasterboard Tienjin, Knauf Gips and Taishan gypsum. You can also send a drywall sample to the lab to be tested for dangerous levels of sulfur. This is the best method but can be expensive. A third option is to use advanced infrared imaging analysis to determine the contaminants in the drywall.[6]

Deleterious health effects from Chinese drywall are respiratory irritation, headaches, sinusitis, eye irritation, throat irritation, malaise/weakness and others. These are consistent with known health effects of sulfur gases such as hydrogen sulfide. It is also common knowledge in the field of medicine that anything that irritates the respiratory tract can aggravate asthma or cause an asthma attack.[7]

TOXIC PRODUCTS AND BAD BUSINESS FROM COMMUNIST CHINA

The U.S. Consumer Product Safety Commission and the U.S. Department of Housing and Urban Development have suggested the following remediation guidance for homes with problem drywall. The following should be replaced.

1. Possible problem drywall.

2. Fire safety alarm devices, including smoke alarms and carbon monoxide alarms.

3. Switches and circuit breakers, and in some cases wiring.

4. Gas service piping and fire suppression sprinkling systems.[8]

This actually means that the entire inside part of the house has to be gutted and all the above items replaced. During this time inhabitants of the house cannot be living there due to the extensive renovations necessary. Also, homeowner's insurance will most likely not cover such remodeling and renovation, and the owners of the house need to contact and likely sue the builder or contactor, who in turn has to sue the Chinese drywall manufacturer. This results in unbelievably complex legal litigation that can take years to rectify with very large attorney bills and no assurance that the litigation will be successful. Many families and individuals may not have the means to support a second the residence while making mortgage payments on their primary residence. Replacing all the drywall in a house typically costs between $80,000 to $100,000.[9] Replacing damaged air conditioners, fire alarms, and switches may result in additional costs. Also,

during this time, it would be impossible to sell the house,
since it needs to be reconstructed from inside out. This
could lead to missing mortgage payments and defaulting
on the mortgage. Banks or other lenders would then need
to repossess the defective house. Also, after successful
remodeling, the owner of the house would have to notify a
potential buyer that this house had toxic drywall installed
initially, which probably would lower the sales value of that
house.

Tainted Chinese drywall is no longer sold in the
United States since the 2012 passage of the Drywall Safety
Act, which set chemical standards for domestic and
imported drywall.[10] However, homeowners who know
they have installed Chinese drywall, or who are
encountering the problems described above, should be
wary.

CHAPTER 3
TOXIC CHINESE FLOORCOVERING

If you were lucky enough to escape having toxic Chinese drywall installed in your house, that does not mean you are home free. You may be at risk from toxic Chinese floorboards.

Floorboard that contains an unacceptably high level of formaldehyde is another example of a toxic product imported from China.

With over 360 stores in North America, Lumber Liquidators is the continent's largest retailer of hardwood flooring. They install more than 100 million square feet of laminate flooring every year, and earn around $1 billion. But according to a "60 Minutes" report from commentator Anderson Cooper, some of their laminate flooring is made in China and may contain health-endangering levels of formaldehyde. The company claims that the flooring it buys from China is safe, but the "60 Minutes" investigation, and testing by the Hardwood, Plywood, and Veneer Association [HPVA], an industrial association that represents some Canadian and American flooring companies, says otherwise. HPVA's testing found a high level of formaldehyde in Chinese floorboards. "We went into a retail store and grabbed a sample, tested it, and six out of eight flunked," said Kip Howlett, president of HPVA.[2]

Why is a high level of formaldehyde a problem? The World Health Organization classifies formaldehyde as a carcinogen, and according to Ed Perratore of Consumer Reports, "At even lower levels formaldehyde can irritate eyes, nose, throat, and skin or trigger an asthma attack in asthma sufferers. And worker exposure to high levels over many years has been linked to ear, nose, and throat cancer, and leukemia." Perratore adds that children and the elderly are at highest risk of adverse health effects from formaldehyde, and that people with respiratory problems also have elevated risks. [3]

How does one know if the laminated flooring one buys is safe? The Environmental Protection Agency recommended that "consumers look for products that are labeled TSCA Title VI compliant. Composite wood products and finished goods containing regulated composite wood products are required to be labeled as such by one year after the final rule is issued."[4] The good news is that stores, including Lowes, have started to halt sales of Chinese-made laminate flooring.[5] Lumber Liquidators also relented, saying, "We have strengthened our quality assurance procedures, launched the largest

voluntary testing program in our nation's history and, in
May 2015, voluntarily suspended the sale of all laminate
flooring from China." The company paid the California
Air Resources Board $2.5 million, which was deposited in
the California Air Pollution Control fund. The fund is
designated for improving California's air quality research
and other projects.[6]

Any time a toxic product that can harm people is
on the market, lawsuits arise. A class action suit brought
against Lumber Liquidators resulted in a $36 million
settlement in October of 2017.[7, 8]

What can you do about toxic flooring that is
already installed? Companies advertise that they will do
testing and, if necessary, replace the flooring--for a fee.[9]
However, you should have the cost of the replacement
covered by the company that sold you the defective
floorcovering.

CHAPTER 4
TOXIC CHINESE MILK

You may say, "Why worry about something that happened with milk in China years ago?" Even though the US does not import milk from China, Chinese milk is used in the manufacturing of some candy, and that candy is then imported into the USA. Therefore, it does matter that Chinese milk was toxic in the past.

It is sad when pets die due to contaminated food, but it is much worse when children and adults die due to contaminated food or medicine. In China there have been two such sad events with altered or contaminated milk and baby formula. The first one, in 2004, concerned fake milk, and the second one, which concerned melamine-contaminated milk, started in 2008.

The 2004 scam led to the death of several dozen babies in rural China. They died of malnutrition after being fed fake baby milk powder that contained very little

nutritional value.[1] The fake formula was distributed by
several companies, and 100-200 babies developed what
doctors in China initially diagnosed as a condition they
called "big head disease," where the infants developed
oversized heads and shrunken limbs. Eventually it was
determined that the children were suffering from severe
malnutrition. The Oriental Morning Post in Shanghai
reported that 50-60 infants died as a result of the deficient
formula.[2]

The second incident affected even more people.
Milk products were found to be contaminated with
melamine, a chemical used in industry to make plastics,
fertilizer, and concrete.[3] In 2010, the BBC reported that,
"Chinese food safety officials have seized 64 tons of raw
dairy material contaminated with the toxic industrial
chemical melamine. The Chinese state news agency,
Xinhua, reported that the quality watchdog in Qinghai
province took the material from a dairy plant there and
that, "Test samples showed the milk powder carried up to
500 times the maximum allowed level of the chemical."[4]

This was a malicious and deceitful action by many
individuals and companies to increase profit by diluting the
milk and adding melamine. In laboratory tests, melamine
mimics protein, so tests would then show that the protein
content of the milk was within normal range when tested,
when in reality it was not. [5]

A leading Chinese dairy company, Sanlu, admitted
that its baby formula was tainted by the chemical
melamine. Investigators traced the adulterated milk to
merchants who served as middlemen between Sanlu and

farmers who produced the milk. The recall, however, was not started until five weeks later, as Chinese authorities delayed making a public announcement. Sanlu executives also suspected that the company's milk supply may have been intentionally sabotaged.[6]

In the end, 300,000 children were made sick by the tainted milk, and at least six children died. An international recall was instituted; 19 people were jailed and two people--a dairy farmer and a milk salesman--were executed because of their role in tainting the milk. But for many, the most outrageous aspect of the entire incident was the attempted cover-up and the slow pace of the recall.[7]

In closing, it may be best to avoid any food products from China, such as candy, that may contain milk.

CHAPTER 5
Toxic Chinese Pet Food

It is sad, and maddening, that a lot of Chinese pet food imported into the USA in the past was adulterated with the toxic chemical melamine. Dogs and cats are an important part of many families in the USA and the rest of the world. When a family dog or cat gets sick and has to be taken to a veterinarian, the family must usually pay all fees for service, since pet medical insurance has only recently been introduced. A pet's illness therefore has a large emotional and financial impact on the family it lives with.

Beginning in March 2007, pet food from Chinese companies was recalled from North America, Europe, and South Africa when consumers reported kidney failure and even death in pets who had eaten the food. The problem was eventually traced back to contaminated wheat, rice, and corn gluten used in pet food.[1] Cornell University and the FDA determined that melamine was present in the pet food,[2] and had been intentionally added to artificially raise the apparent level of protein in the feed, just as with the tainted milk discussed in the previous chapter. [3] Then, a second chemical additive was discovered. On May 8, 2007 the New York Times reported that animal feed producers in China often purchased the chemical cyanuronic acid. According to the Chinese chemical makers who sold the acid, this chemical was often added to animal feed, again to raise the apparent protein levels. [3]

After these chemical adulterants had been identified, the largest pet food recall in history took place. About 180 different brands of pet food were included in the recall, in part because an amazing variety of different brands of dog and cat food and treats used the same tainted ingredients from the same suppliers. Some of these brands were listed as top quality brands and sold at a high price, and others were discount brands, yet all used some of the same ingredients. [4] In late April 2007, Chinese authorities acknowledged for the first time that the toxic chemicals were present in the pet food, and began cooperating with the recall efforts, though they denied that melamine was necessarily the cause of the pet illnesses and deaths being reported. [5]

When there is damage to people, property or pets, there are also lawsuits and settlements. More than 20,000 pet owners took part in class action suits as a result of the 2007 recall, and eventually a $24 million settlement was awarded. Half of this money went to the pet owners, and half of it went to lawyers' fees and other expenses. [4]

More recently, in 2014, the FDA reported that more than 1,000 dogs have died as the result of toxic jerky treats imported from China, and issued a warning about the treats.[6] So in spite of the problem of toxic Chinese dog and cat food being identified in March 2007, the problem persisted until 2014, resulting in the death of more animals. In May 2014, Purina and Waggin' Train LLC agreed to create a $6.5 million fund to compensate pet owners whose animals may have been harmed by contaminated treats, and also agreed to increase their quality assurance testing—but both companies stopped short of conceding that their products contained any toxic additives.[7]

According to reporting by CBSNews.com, some of the symptoms pets show after consuming food contaminated with melamine or similar toxins are as follows: "decreased appetite, decreased activity, vomiting, diarrhea (sometimes with blood or mucus), increased water consumption and/or increased urination. In severe cases, pets may be diagnosed with pancreatitis, gastrointestinal bleeding, and kidney failure."[8]

It may be best to avoid buying pet food manufactured in China in view of this past history of malfeasance.

CHAPTER 6
Toxic Chinese Heparin

When a patient goes to a hospital or a doctor's office there is an expectation that any drugs administered are safe and unadulterated. Unfortunately, that was not true about heparin manufactured in China in the past. Heparin is a drug that is used as an anticoagulant (blood thinner) and is administered by injection. For example, following hip or knee replacement surgery, heparin is administered to lessen the chance of a serious complication called deep vein thrombosis, also known as blood clots in the veins. In 2008 there were reports of serious injury and even death as a result of heparin produced in China.[1]

Changzhou SPL, a Chinese subsidiary of the American company Scientific Protein Laboratories, produced the raw heparin components. These were then sold to Baxter Healthcare Corporation, which created the final product administered to patients.[2] It was those initial raw components that later proved to be tainted. The FDA

received nearly 800 reports of serious side effects
associated with the drug, including difficulty breathing,
rapidly falling blood pressure, and shock.[3] At least 81
people died as a result of the contaminated heparin. In
subsequent Congressional hearings, the FDA intimated
that the heparin may have been deliberately tampered with,
as up to one third of the material in some of the heparin
was contaminants. The contaminant in this case was a
compound called oversulfated chondroitin sulfate. David
G. Strunce, Scientific Protein Laboratories' chief executive,
also claimed that the Chinese government stymied his
company's investigations into the source of the toxic
additives.[2]

The heparin fraud worked by diluting heparin with
oversulfated chondroitin sulfate, a chemical that costs only
one percent of what heparin would, but which mimics
heparin in lab tests.[2] In addition to the illness and death of
patients, this also resulted in economic loss to Baxter
Healthcare Corporation, the eventual distributer of the
tainted heparin products, and a stain on its reputation. In
February 2008, the company recalled several of its heparin
products as a result of the deaths caused by tainted
heparin.[4]

The problem was not limited to the United States.
The following month, the FDA published information to
help researchers detect batches of contaminated heparin,
and batch recalls began in Germany. Other European
countries and Japan followed suit. In all, at least 11
countries identified contaminated heparin supplies in use.[5]

Throughout this stage of the process, Chinese officials maintained that the contaminants had not caused adverse health effects and death among patients who used them. One Chinese official suggested that contamination of the finished vials, produced in America, might instead be to blame, and that any future inspection of Chinese drug manufacturing facilities should include a reciprocal inspection of the American facilities.[5]

The FDA needs to be given a bigger budget to be able to test medications imported from China, to decrease the likelihood that an incident like this will happen again.

CHAPTER 7
Problems with Chinese Vaccines

The introduction of vaccinations has been a major step forward in medicine to prevent or attenuate a variety of bacterial and viral diseases. In most countries, vaccines have been relatively well accepted. Recently, however, anti-vaccine movements have gained traction. Therefore, it is very sad that there was a scandal in China involving the use of expired and improperly stored vaccines. This in turn has created a suspicion among Chinese citizens that vaccinations are not safe, even though they are when properly administered. The incidence of complications with vaccinations is very low. However, here is the story of China's vaccine problems.

In 2016, almost $90 million-worth of improperly stored vaccines were distributed in China, across a wide swath of the country. Once this came to light, Chinese citizens were further enraged because the Chinese authorities knew about the problem for nearly a year

before making a public announcement about the faulty
vaccines.[1]

     The history of problems with vaccines in China
goes back longer than this scandal. According to Radio
Free Asia [RFA], referencing a report from the China
Economic Times, in just one province, improperly stored
vaccines killed four children and caused illness in more
than 70 others between 2006 and 2008. RFA also reports
that in 2011, problems with a mandatory measles vaccine
resulted in the death of one child and illness in others. And
in 2014, 17 babies died after receiving the hepatitis B
vaccine. Although the authorities denied that the 2014
deaths were caused by the vaccine, parents were convinced
otherwise. Finally, in 2015 nearly 400 children in Henan
province developed severe health problems after being
given expired vaccines.[2]

     The vaccines reported in 2016 were dangerous for
the same reason—they had been improperly stored, being
kept in an "overheated, dilapidated storeroom," according
to the New York Times. The main suspect in their
distribution, a hospital pharmacist, had already been
convicted of illegally selling vaccines in 2009.[3] The
vaccines were purchased from both legal and illegal
sources, and then sold to illegal agents as well as legitimate
disease control centers.[4] Eventually, 130 people were
arrested in connection with the illegal vaccine trade.[5]

     Fortunately, it is unlikely that the improperly-
stored vaccines caused serious health problems. According
to the World Health Organization, vaccines that have not
been correctly stored may become less effective, but they

are seldom dangerous. Still, Chinese citizens were shocked
and angered by their government's response to the crisis.
Not only did officials delay informing the public, but
through the subsequent investigation it came to light that
there were very few government employees properly
trained to inspect vaccines and drugs and thereby prevent
similar problems in the future.[6]

It is also wrong that parents who express their
concerns about the vaccine scandals may be harassed or
imprisoned. One parent who had planned to take part in
protests that followed the 2016 incident said, "I was
forcibly escorted home by officials from my
hometown…Now they're watching us 24 hours a day."[6]

The Chinese government has a habit of
suppressing bad news. Scandals like this one lead to fewer
people getting vaccinations for their children, leaving them
unprotected. It is very difficult for health professionals to
regain public trust once that trust has been lost.

Since vaccines need to be properly stored and
used before their expiration date, we should not be using
vaccines manufactured in China, given what transpired
there.

CHAPTER 8
Toxic Toothpaste and Cough Syrup

Toxic toothpaste is another example of how some Chinese companies substitute a toxic ingredient for a safe ingredient in order to produce their product more cheaply and increase their profit margin. Glycerin is a safe food additive used to thicken toothpaste. However, some Chinese companies have used diethylene glycol, which is cheaper but also toxic, as a substitute for glycerin. [1]

In 2007, US federal health officials advised consumers to throw away all toothpaste produced in China, after Chinese toothpaste containing diethylene glycol was found in Miami, Los Angeles, and Puerto Rico.[1] Although no deaths were reported, thousands of tubes of toothpaste were removed from store shelves. [2] The contaminated toothpaste was a worldwide problem affecting many countries such as Canada, Australia, New Zealand, Saudi Arabia, and European Union countries.[3, 4] In the EU, a consumer alert system allowed all member states to rapidly remove two brands of toothpaste containing diethylene glycol shortly after they were first discovered in Spain. [4] The Royal Canadian Mounted Police warned the public that swallowing the contaminated toothpaste could cause reactions from nausea and dizziness to kidney failure, coma, and even death. At the same time, counterfeit Colgate toothpaste contaminated with bacteria was also found and pulled from shelves in Canada. [5] To provide worldwide distribution of a toxic product shows a callous disregard for people's safety throughout the world.

In spite of the evidence of diethylene glycol in Chinese manufactured toothpaste, Chinese regulators reported that their investigation of the toothpaste companies uncovered no wrongdoing. The regulators also disputed whether small amounts of diethylene glycol were in fact dangerous. However, the FDA maintains that this substance cannot be safely used in toothpaste in any amount.[1]

Toxic Cold Medicine

In 2006, Panama's Ministry of Health found toxic diethylene glycol used in cold medicine to be the cause of 46 deaths. They traced the diethylene glycol back to the Taixing Glycerine Factory, a Chinese company that had falsely labeled the diethylene glycol as glycerin. A government agency in Panama then bought the mislabeled chemical and used it to make cold medicine, unaware that they were using a toxic substance. [6] So this is the second toxic product out of China contaminated with toxic diethylene glycol.

It is unconscionable to use a toxic product, a component in antifreeze, and incorporate it in toothpaste and cough syrup, yet Chinese companies did so. Fortunately, the amount in toothpaste did not produce recognizable harm. But toxic cough syrup killed many people in Panama.

CHAPTER 9
Problems with Some Chinese Foods

The problems with Chinese food are so numerous that it is impossible to cover them all. One may say, "Who cares? I do not plan to travel to China, so why worry?" Please remember that China is our biggest trading partner and is buying up a lot of US companies, so the food we eat, such as shrimp, fish, ginger etc. may be coming from China. When one goes to a Chinese restaurant, one is frequently asked if one wants white rice or fried rice with one's meal. A better question may be, "Do you want your rice with cadmium or without?"

In most countries, one of the functions of the government is to ensure that the food is safe to eat, the water is clean to drink, and the air is clean to breathe. Unfortunately, China's supervision of the food industry is very slipshod and some of the businessmen in the food industry are unscrupulously putting profits above food safety. There are so many problems in the food industry that covering it would take a separate book, so in this chapter we will cover problems with candy, rice, ginger, honey, eggs, cooking oil, vinegar, watermelons, buns, beans, and dumplings. Problems with milk products and pet foods were already covered in a separate chapter. Also, a separate chapter will be devoted to problems with meat and seafood.

Contaminated Candy

I will cover problems with contaminated candy first. In September 2007, authorities in the Philippines found formaldehyde in White Rabbit Creamy Candy, a brand of candy produced in China and sold internationally. The following year, the New Zealand government found toxic melamine (discussed in earlier chapters) in the same candy.[1]

In 2012, The Center for Environmental Health released a report showing that some ginger- and plum-flavored candies produced in China contained more than 60 times the amount of lead allowed by FDA limits. While it is not possible to tell through this testing how the candy came to have such a high lead content, it could be a result of processing, storage, or even packaging.[2]

So, when is a lot of candy consumed in the US? Halloween of course. In 2008, Natural News put out the following warning: "This Halloween, children across the United States may be poisoned with toxic melamine, a potentially deadly chemical that causes severe kidney damage, liver damage, and even death. This chemical is found in chocolates and candy products made in China, which is now embroiled in a global melamine scandal involving eggs, animal feed, candies, infant formula, milk products and much more."[3]

The previously reviewed articles covered 2008 to

2015. It would be best to not eat candy manufactured in
China.

Toxic Rice

Contaminated rice is a huge problem in China.
Chinese citizens make rice a daily staple in their diet in
much the same way consumers in the US value bread,
Italians value pasta, and Germans value potatoes. To tell
Chinese people that their rice is toxic is like telling
Americans that their bread is toxic. How could this
happen? The contamination of the rice occurs by the soil
the rice is grown in being contaminated with cadmium.
For example, Hunan province is China's largest producer
of rice and cadmium. In this case, the cadmium is released
by metal smelting factories. Cadmium is a heavy metal and
accumulates in the body, causing various health problems,
from emphysema to cancer. In some farms in Hunan
province, the level of cadmium found in the rice crops is
more than 50 percent above the limit allowed by the
Chinese government (a limit that is similar to international
standards) as a result of cadmium pollution from
factories.[4]

As if cadmium contamination were not bad
enough, there are instances of arsenic contaminating the
soil and crops. Poor regulation of factories has led to
widespread contamination of waterways in China, and this
in turn has led to contaminated crops. For instance, an
arsenic mine in Yunnan province was found to have left
the slag from its mines exposed, allowing the arsenic to
seep into the water supply and ultimately into crops. As a
result, according to The Epoch Times, "The arsenic
content found in crops and nearby regions is over 100

times higher than the recommended safety level. Untreated industrial wastewater containing excessive heavy metals is also discharged into rivers, onto land, and passed to rice crops through irrigation." Even more alarming is that farmers have been complaining about the pollution for many years, but authorities have not intervened.[5]

Part of the problem with heavy metals such as cadmium, arsenic, and lead contaminating soil in China is that there is no practical way of cleaning up the soil. Therefore, it is a permanent contamination of the topsoil. China already has a short supply of land for agricultural use to feed its population. There is no reasonable way to remove the contaminated topsoil and replace it with new, good topsoil.

Dangerous Ginger

Another way crops can be contaminated and made toxic is by spraying them with toxic pesticides. That is what happened with Chinese ginger. In July 2007, high levels of aldicarb sulfoxide, a dangerous pesticide, were found in ginger imported from China. Small amounts of this pesticide can cause nausea and blurred vision,[6] while 50 mg is enough to kill a 110-lb person, according to some experts.[7]

Tainted Chinese Honey

When people think of honey, they imagine a natural, healthy food. Some people even prefer it to granulated sugar as a healthy alternative sweetener. Americans eat about 1.3 pounds of honey per person each year, and honey is an ingredient in many processed foods such as sauces and cereals. However, American beekeepers can supply only about half the honey the US market consumes, so the rest must be imported.[8]

It turns out that China is the biggest supplier of honey for the US market, but that honey can be contaminated with antibiotics, lead, or can even be fake honey. In 2001, Chinese beekeepers began using an antibiotic called chloramphenicol in their beehives to combat a bacterial disease called Foulbrood Disease. However, chloramphenicol can be fatal to a small percentage of the population. In addition to pesticide use, lead-contaminated honey is produced when beekeepers store the honey they harvest in containers with lead soldering. And finally, some Chinese honey brokers create fake "honey" by combining sugar water with thickeners, sweeteners, and artificial flavors. [9]

Since tainted Chinese honey has been banned from entering the US, Chinese companies sometimes "launder" their honey through other nations including India, Vietnam, and Malaysia.[9]

Chinese Egg Problems

Problems with Chinese eggs fall into three categories: melamine contamination, fake eggs, and preserved eggs.

In 2008, officials in Hong Kong found that eggs produced by one Chinese company, Dalian Hanwei Enterprise Group, contained melamine levels of 4.7 parts per million, almost double the legal standard of 2.5 parts per million. The discovery came on the heels of the milk contamination scandal discussed in Chapter 4, and led to concern about whether other food products were similarly contaminated. There was also the question of how the melamine had entered the eggs. Officials hypothesized that the chickens' feed may have contained melamine.[10, 11]

In addition to contaminated eggs, some eggs sold in China were found to be outright fakes. It strains the imagination that anybody would conceive the idea to make fake eggs to earn crooked money, but it did happen. The ingredients for fake eggs are cheaper than the cost of a real egg and therefore there is a higher profit margin. In 2012 Time Magazine, picking up on reporting in the Guangming Daily, reported that shoppers in Chinese markets were discovering that some "eggs" they had purchased were actually made from a mixture of algae-based coagulants, starch, resin, and pigment. After creating egg "whites" and "yolks" from this mixture, the counterfeiters then poured the fake eggs into artificial shells made of wax, calcium carbonate, and gypsum powder.[12] Hoaxorfact.com even reported that some unscrupulous entrepreneurs were offering seminars in how to create the fake eggs so that others could follow in their footsteps! One professor at Hong Kong Chinese University warned that some of the eggs contained alum (a sulfate), and said that long-term consumption of this material could lead to dementia.[13]

The last item to cover regarding Chinese eggs is cheating on preserved eggs. According to the South China Morning Post, some Chinese manufacturers were using a "short cut" process to create preserved duck eggs, sometimes called "thousand year eggs," which are a popular food in China. The eggs are typically preserved for about two months in a mixture of baking soda, salt, and quicklime, but unscrupulous manufacturers were instead curing them in copper sulfate. This cut the curing time in half, to only one month, and lowered costs, thereby benefitting manufacturers. Unfortunately, copper sulfate also contains high levels of heavy metals such as arsenic and lead, so it is not suitable for use in food.[14]

Gutter Oil

"Gutter oil" is a term used in China (and some other parts of Asia) to describe cooking oil that has been collected from illegal and often unsanitary sources. While some of the oil is recycled from restaurant fryers, some is rendered fat from slaughterhouses and sewage, and the various kinds of recycled oil are typically mixed together to create the "gutter oil." This is then sold to street food vendors and small, cheap restaurants at a much lower price than clean cooking oil, and can make patrons sick with symptoms such as diarrhea. There are also concerns that the oil may contain high levels of carcinogens that could lead to liver cancer over time.[15]

Though the Chinese government has outlawed gutter oil and is trying to stop its production, in 2013 the Washington Post reported that a large gutter oil production ring with over 100 people was discovered. More than 3,000 tons of gutter oil were seized, and it is estimated that the ring members had already sold $1.6 million of oil at the time of the bust. [16]

Toxic Vinegar

In 2011, 11 people died and 120 more were sickened after consuming vinegar that had been stored in antifreeze barrels. The vinegar was used to prepare a large communal Ramadan meal.[17] As discussed above, unsanitary or unsafe methods of food storage have led to a number of problems with food in China.

Bursting Watermelons

Sometimes the problems with food in China come from misuse of legal pesticides and fertilizers. In 2011, some farmers suffered an epidemic of bursting watermelons after they administered the growth chemical forchlorfenuron to their crops too late in the growing process. While this is a legal food drug and is also used in the United States, it was not meant to be used in this way.[18] Fortunately, the results were not toxic or harmful in this case, but the farmers did lose many acres of crops.

Tainted Steamed Buns

In 2015, two factories in China were found to be selling steamed buns that contained high levels of chemicals. One of the companies had used artificial colorings and flavorings to replace corn, and was also steaming the buns in outdoor tents that contained mud and mold.[19]

Toxic Bean-Sprouts and Beans

In April 2011, bean sprouts in the Chinese city of Shenyang were found to be treated with sodium nitrate, antibiotics, and plant hormones to make them grow faster. Forty tons of bean sprouts were confiscated when this was discovered. And in 2010, 3.5 tons of green beans that had been grown with isocarbophos, a prohibited pesticide, were destroyed in the Chinese city of Wuhan.[20]

Aluminum-Contaminated Dumplings

In 2016, several dumpling restaurants in China were shut down after health inspectors found that their dumplings contained high levels of aluminum. The aluminum originated from an aluminum-rich baking powder used to make the dumplings, which the owner of one of the stores said gave the buns a softer texture.[21] While aluminum was for many years a common ingredient in baking powder, even in the United States,[22] the baking powder used in the dumpling restaurants contained an unacceptably high level of aluminum, and some of the proprietors had already been warned against using it on earlier occasions.[21]

So what are we to learn from all this? First, when traveling in China, eat only in first class restaurants and especially ones located in good hotels that cater to tourists. Second, when buying produce and food here in the USA, try to avoid food imported from China.

CHAPTER 10
Problems with Chinese Meat and Seafood

Meat or seafood is usually the main course of a meal. Therefore, though I have already discussed some problems with Chinese food, problems with meat and seafood in China deserve a separate chapter. Problems with meat can fall into the following categories: outdated meat, toxic chemicals and/or antibiotics in meat, bacterial and viral contamination, and mislabeled meat.

Outdated Meat

In 2014, the Chinese branch of OSI Group, an American company, came under investigation for selling expired meat. The group was accused of repackaging the meat with new labels and new expiration dates, and selling it to customers within China that included giant chains like McDonalds, KFC, Pizza Hut, and Burger King. Those chains stopped using the meat after Dragon TV (a Shanghai television station) ran an expose on OSI Group. The case went to court, and in 2016 the Shanghai

Municipal Food and Drug Administration fined OSI $2.5
million and sent 10 of its employees to jail.[1]

Toxic Chemicals and Antibiotics in Meat

There have been numerous cases of meat found
to be adulterated with toxic chemicals or banned additives.
Here are just a few examples:

In 2011, some samples of condensed pigs' blood
sold in China were found to contain formaldehyde, which
is toxic. While pigs' blood is not commonly used in
American cooking, it is a common ingredient in China and
essential in making some traditional dishes.[2]

The Chinese government, in explaining its
difficulties in combatting widespread food adulteration,
described a company in Mongolia that was caught with 23
tons of fake beef jerky and other meat that was full of
bacteria, and a group in Guizhau Province caught with 8.8
tons of toxic chicken feet marinated with hydrogen
peroxide.[3]

In 2012, some chicken sold by KFC in China was
found to have high levels of antibiotics and hormones.[4]

Excessive antibiotic use in food animals is a
widespread problem in China. The country uses about
80,000 tons of antibiotics for livestock every year, as
opposed to 10,000 tons in the United States. [5]

Bacterial and Viral Contamination of Meat

According to a 2014 report from the online site
Food Safety News, "Shuanghui International, China's

biggest meat products company (which purchased
Smithfield Foods in 2013 for $4.7 billion), has been
plagued by constant reports here in China of meat infested
with maggots, customers succumbing to food poisoning,
and random testing that shows illegal levels of bacteria and
illegal additives such as clenbuterol in their meat."[6] But this
is far from the only company with food safety problems.
There have also been reports of Chinese pork that glows
blue because (according to the Shanghai Health
Supervision Department) it is infested with
phosphorescent bacteria,[7] and between April 2013 and July
2014, 150 people died of avian flu as the result of
unsanitary conditions in the country's poultry markets.[8]

Mislabeled Meat

In addition to problems with adulteration and
food poisoning, there have also been a number of cases of
meat from some animals being intentionally mislabeled as
other types of meat. For instance, according to the New
York Times (drawing on a statement from China's
Ministry of Public Security), "Sixty-three people [in China]
were arrested and accused of 'buying fox, mink and rat and
other meat products that had not undergone inspection,'
which they doused in gelatin, red pigment and nitrates, and
sold as mutton in Shanghai and adjacent Jiangsu Province
for about $1.6 million."[9] And it seems that no companies
are too big to be duped in China. Walmart in China
recalled packages of "five spice donkey meat" after
learning that the meat in the packages contained DNA
from other animals, possibly including fox meat again.[10]

Problems with Chinese Seafood

Why should there be problems in the USA with
Chinese seafood? China one of the largest exporters of
seafood to the US, and in fact produces 62 percent of the
world's farmed seafood.[11] " So if we are importing a large
amount of seafood from China, then China's seafood
problems become our seafood problems. As with many of
the other problems discussed above, the problems with
Chinese seafood are often a matter of poor quality control.
In 2007, the FDA became so concerned with the levels of
carcinogens and antibiotics repeatedly found in imported
Chinese seafood that it temporarily banned imports of
some types of fish from China. Some of the fish was just
plain dirty, while other samples tested contained veterinary
drugs or salmonella.[12] Some of the fish contained
chemicals intended to help treat fish diseases caused by
living in dirty water; unfortunately, these same chemicals
can be dangerous and unhealthy for humans to consume.[13]
These included, according to ABC news, "the
antimicrobials nitrofuran, malachite green, gentian violet,
and fluoroquinolones. Nitrofuran malachite green and
gentian violet are used to treat fungal infections, but have
been shown to be carcinogenic with long-term exposure in
lab animals."[14] As an article published in The Lancet in
2013 put it, "Since water is essential to food production,
preparation, and processing, a major source of foodborne
disease in China stems from the shortage of clean water
and poor sanitation."[15]

Due to all of the examples mentioned above,
consumers should exercise caution when purchasing meat
and seafood from China.

CHAPTER 11
Toxic Clothing from China

Most people are aware of air and water pollution and are also aware that there can be occasional problems with adulterated food. But who would ever think that clothing that we buy and wear can be harmful? The main toxic culprit in clothing from China is formaldehyde. The role of formaldehyde is to protect clothes from wrinkling and shrinking. However, there is controversy both in the lay and scientific literature as to whether or not there is a problem with formaldehyde in clothing.

In 1992, Fowler, Skinner and Belsito published an article in the Journal of the American Academy of Dermatology entitled "Allergic contact dermatitis from formaldehyde resins in permanent press clothing: an underdiagnosed cause of contact dermatitis," which found that some people have an allergic reaction to the formaldehyde used in clothing.[1] A more recent study, published in 2010, suggests that this may not be a problem for most people. The study by Ac De Groot et al.,

39

published in the journal Contact Dermatitis, states, "The
amount of free formaldehyde in most garments will likely
be below the threshold for elicitation of dermatitis for all
but most sensitive patients."[2] However, Alternative-za-
vas.com reported that "In clothes manufactured in China
and Southeast Asia, the investigators found 100 to 500
times higher levels of formaldehyde than the level which is
considered to be medically safe."[3] And a 2010 research
review by the U.S. Government Accountability Office
found that formaldehyde in clothing can cause a range of
symptoms from nausea to asthma attacks, and that long-
term exposure is even linked to tumor growth. [4] The same
report says that while the American Apparel and Footwear
Association has advised that formaldehyde levels should
be undetectable in clothing intended for infants and
toddlers, and at or below 75 parts per million in clothing
for children over age three and for adults, some items
produced in China and sold in the United States had
formaldehyde levels of up to 206 parts per million.

Some have suggested that the formaldehyde level
can be reduced by washing the clothing, but others dispute
that. Consumers should be conscious of the possibility of
formaldehyde when buying clothing made in China, and
should also re-think buying wrinkle-resistant clothing,
since formaldehyde is used to make it wrinkle-resistant.[5]

CHAPTER 12
TOXIC CHINESE TOYS

Toys manufactured in China can contain toxic materials. The main culprit is lead, but other offenders can be cadmium, arsenic, bromide, mercury, and plastics, such as phthalates. According to the website Poisoned Pets, "A Chinese consumer organization recently warned Chinese parents to not let children put toys in their mouths after many were found to contain a toxic agent that could cause liver or kidney damage."[1] It is easy to give such advice, but impossible to follow it. You may be inclined at this point to say, "Let us buy toys from reputable, large U.S. companies." That really does not work. For example, in 2007, toy manufacturer Mattel issued a recall of nearly seven million toys manufactured in China, due to dangers posed by high levels of lead in the toys.[2]

Lead contamination can take on two forms: lead in the product itself and lead paint on top of the toy surface. According to reporting by Forbes, a consumer safety group tested over a thousand children's toys using handheld devices and found many that contained lead, arsenic, mercury, and other dangerous substances. Children's jewelry was especially bad, with 15 percent of products tested found to have lead levels above 600 parts per million.[3] Across the board, about 3 percent of toys in this test were found to have dangerous levels of chemicals, sometimes prompting recalls. For instance, a manufacturer of Thomas the Train toys had to recall 1.5 million toys because they were colored with lead paint.[4] Similar testing conducted in China by Greenpeace and IPEN (an organization that works to eliminate toxic chemicals in products) found that 32.6 percent of toys being sold in China were tainted. The worst product in that particular test was a toy ring that contained, according to reporting by The Telegraph, "more than the 1200 times the amount of lead permitted under European safety standards."[5]

Why worry about lead in toys? Lead exposure can lead to a variety of health problems in children, including learning disabilities and kidney failure. And children are especially at risk because they often chew on toys.[6] Parentsmap.com has warned that there is no safe threshold for lead exposure in the children and, that, if possible, they should not come in contact with it.[6]

Following lead, cadmium is the next most frequently used heavy metal in Chinese manufactured toys. Cadmium is also a carcinogen and affects children in much the same way lead does. It is especially common in costume jewelry. According to an Associated Press investigation of jewelry purchased in New York,

California, Texas, and Ohio, "A lab analysis revealed that the most contaminated trinket contained 91 per cent cadmium by weight, while other objects tested at dangerous levels including 87 percent, 86 percent and 84 percent by weight. Twelve percent of the pieces contained at least 10 percent cadmium" (as reported by the New York Daily News).[7]

Arsenic is also mentioned often as a toxic contaminant in toys, but specific data and analysis is missing. Since arsenic is a strong poison, it would not take much to make a child sick.

In addition to heavy metal contamination of toys, toys made out of plastic can be contaminated with phthalates. This applies both to children's toys and to pet toys. Phthalates are a chemical compound added to plastic to make it more flexible, but they can have serious health consequences if ingested. Poisoned Pets states that in a study performed by the Consumer Council, phthalates were found in over half the children's toys tested, sometimes at levels up to 300 times that allowed by US standards. China does not regulate the use of phthalates in toys or pet products, but in Europe and the US toys can contain no more than 0.1 percent phthalates. Testing of pet toys also found that 45 percent of them contained detectable levels of lead. [1]

Rather than apologize for all these tainted products, Chinese authorities, according to Wikipedia, ordered that a story about tainted Chinese products be removed from copies of Time Magazine sold in China,[8] and other negative reports may also have been censored.

Chinese officials have blamed Western media agencies for
the bad press, an accusation which this author finds
preposterous.

CHAPTER 13
Chinese Hacking and Industrial Espionage

Nobody is immune to hacking. Hacking can affect large
companies or organizations such as Sony, Equifax, or the
Democratic Party, and medium and small businesses such
as hospitals and dental offices that are then extorted for
ransom money.

The countries that engage most heavily in hacking
are China, Russia, and the USA, but there are plenty of
other countries that participate in hacking, including Iran
and North Korea.[1] A comprehensive summary of hacking
by China can be found under the "Cyberwarfare in China"
article in Wikipedia.[2] According to this article, China
utilizes military hacking units, specialists in its Ministries of
State Security and Public Security, and also civilian groups
to engage in hacking.

Some high-profile cases serve to illustrate the aims
of Chinese hacking. In May 2014, the US District Court in
Pittsburgh, Pennsylvania indicted five Chinese army
officials for computer crimes aimed at Western

Pennsylvania organizations. Those organizations hacked included US Steel, Westinghouse Electric, and Alcoa, as well as the United Steel Workers International Union. According to the Pittsburgh Post-Gazette, the information stolen included "technology secrets, strategies for dealing with Chinese companies, tactics for anti-dumping complaints with the World Trade Organization and lobbying plans."[3]

The United States hacks the Chinese government and Chinese military, but does not steal commercial secrets from Chinese companies. However, the Chinese government and military are actively involved in stealing commercial secrets from U.S. companies and passing them on to Chinese companies. Wang Dong, one of the criminals cited above, sent emails to 30 employees of US Steel Corporation that appeared to come from the company's chief executive, John Surma. When employees clicked on links in the emails or downloaded attached files, they unwittingly opened malware designed to give Wang access to industry secrets and trade negotiation information. All of this occurred while US Steel was in the midst of pressing for sanctions against Chinese-made steel pipes, under allegations of the Chinese government subsidizing production and thereby artificially lowering prices. [4]

Finally, a story that the website Renewable Energy World covered in 2012 was featured in the news program "60 Minutes" in January 2016.[5] The story covered the case of American Superconductors (AMSC), whose intellectual property was stolen by Chinese company Sinovel. One of

AMSC's employees, working from Austria, acted as an inside agent to help the Chinese company steal important technical information. The employee served jail time, but when the Chinese government refused to take any steps to punish or investigate Sinovel, AMSC brought a $1.2 billion civil lawsuit in US court to recover damages.[6] In January 2018, a federal jury found Sinovel guilty.[7]

It is not only U.S. industries that are concerned about China hacking industrial secrets. The German government has warned its industries to fear China's information gathering prowess and take extra precautions against hacking when traveling to China for business.[8]

The hacking also is not limited to businesses. In 2014, Chinese hackers using malware broke into the computer system of the Office of Personnel Management, a government agency that stores the personal data of all federal employees. According to the New York Times, vulnerable information in this hack included "foreign contacts, previous jobs and personal information like past drug use" from federal employees applying for security clearances.[9]

And in 2016, Chinese debuted its J-20 stealth jet fighter, which is believed to be based on stolen blueprints from the U.S. military's F-22 jets.[10] It took many years and a large amount of money for the U.S. to develop stealth airplanes, and by hacking U.S. blueprints China was able to develop the stealth fighters faster and more cheaply.

It pays to hire the best internet security company to minimize the risk of getting hacked, but even then there is no guarantee that one will not get hacked.

CHAPTER 14
Chinese Hacking of the Nuclear and Solar Energy Sector

In an effort to try to get away from coal-fired power plants, China is pursuing nuclear, solar and wind power energy. Unfortunately, hacking was and is an integral part of this effort.

One example involves the Westinghouse Electric Company. In 2010, Westinghouse and the Chinese government were engaged in talks where Westinghouse was voluntarily sharing information on building nuclear reactors. According to this plan, Westinghouse would then build 4 nuclear reactors in China and earn a hefty fee in the process. However, as the negotiations were going on, Chinese military officials were also hacking Westinghouse's computers to steal thousands of pages of documents, according to an indictment filed in the US District Court for Western Pennsylvania.[1] These documents included technical information that would allow Chinese contractors to build nuclear power plants on their own, without hiring Westinghouse to do the job. [2] In

addition to stealing nuclear power plant information
through hacking, China also employed spies. These
included 66-year-old Szuhsing "Allen" Ho, who admitted
to helping a state-owned Chinese nuclear company gain
information about US nuclear technology but said that he
was doing so as part of legal business practice. Ho
recruited retired Westinghouse engineers and other former
Westinghouse employees to act as "consultants" to the
Chinese company. According to reporting by the
Pittsburgh Post-Gazette, "the [US] government has said
that Mr. Ho's consulting services amount to nuclear
espionage and that he was acting as a foreign agent when
he recruited nuclear scientists to educate China's nuclear
engineers on aspects of commercial reactors." [4]

China may also have attempted to gain advantages
in the development of solar power through hacking. The
alleged plan by the Chinese in the area of solar power
technology is as follows. First, hack and get the knowhow,
and then through government-subsidized manufacturers,
under-price other solar panel manufacturers and capture
large segments of the world solar market. Chinese hackers
allegedly stole solar panel technology from Solar World
AG, a German solar power firm. According to the US
Justice Department's case in the matter, hacker Wen Xinyu
hacked into the email of Solar World executives and stole
information from thousands of emails, some of which
would provide inside technical information on designing
solar panels. [5]

In 2014, some key rulings about unfair business
practices in the solar panel market were made by the

United States Commerce Department. The Commerce Department ruled that Chinese solar companies had received unfair subsidies from the Chinese government and that they had been selling their panels below cost, both of which had unfairly driven competing US and European solar companies out of the market. In response, the Commerce Department placed duties of up to 55.49 percent on Chinese-made solar panels.[6] According to reporting by the New York Times, this had an almost immediate effect on American and European solar manufacturers, whose products quickly became more competitive with those of their Chinese counterparts.[6]

CHAPTER 15
Chinese Counterfeiting of CDs and DVDs

China has perfected the art of counterfeiting products of all sorts such as CDs, DVDs, software, watches, purses, clothing, and cell phones. The most visible and prevalent of these products is the counterfeiting of CDs and DVDs. The economic loss to the originators of the material is substantial and worldwide. A musician whose agent puts out a CD does not collect royalties on pirated material and the sales of legitimate CDs are undercut by the cheaper counterfeit CD. This also applies to DVDs. If a movie comes out and at the same time its counterfeit DVD hits the market place, people do not go to the movie theater to see the movie but instead buy the counterfeit DVD. This counterfeiting also harms other countries besides the United States. The EU reports that in 2006, 23 million counterfeit CDs and DVDs were confiscated, 93 percent originating in China.[1]

According to Jeffrey Hays, citing various sources at factsanddetails.com, 95 percent of CD and music sales in China are made through piracy. CDs by Western musicians as well as "popular Chinese revolutionary songs" are sold on the streets, sometimes for as little as 50 cents. Pirated material accounts for 5 percent of the $40-billion-dollar music industry in China, and most of the counterfeit CDs are produced and sold domestically.[2]

The situation is equally bad for movies. In 2007 in China, an estimated 93 percent of movies sold were pirated, most likely due to the availability of counterfeit versions sold on the streets, in subway stations, markets, and backrooms of video stores. The film industries of Hong Kong and Hollywood have lost billions due to this extreme pirating.[2] However, Chinese authorities have taken steps to control and fight counterfeiting. In 2015, the Associated Press reported about a ceremonial event in which customs officers destroyed 16 million pirated CDs and DVDs. [3]

As reported by United Press International (UPI), Zhao Weisui, the Vice Minister of Culture in Nanjing, China, said, "The fight against piracy is a long-term, difficult and complicated cause that demands the joint and continuous endeavors of the government, business sector and all circles of society. We can't afford to underestimate or overlook the problems still plaguing China's audiovisual market."[4] United Press International also writes that "the piracy issue has proven embarrassing for the Chinese government, which has pledged to improve copyright protection as part of its membership in the World Trade Organization." China has increasingly depended upon foreign trading partners, who have been critical of Beijing's efforts. A "shadow economy" has risen due to the extent of pirating in China. According to UPI, "Recent estimates

by international trade groups indicate that piracy in China
directly or indirectly employs three million to five million
people and generates $40 billion to $80 billion every year."
Additionally, every year the movie industry loses
approximately $3 billion in revenue.[4] Those who
knowingly buy counterfeit CDs and DVDs are supporting
an illegal industry just to save a little money.

CHAPTER 16
China's Unfair Business Practices

China's unfair business practices fall into several categories, ranging from currency manipulation to steel and aluminum dumping, from rare earth metal ploys to unfair tariffs.

Chinese Currency Manipulation

Currency manipulation gives a country an unfair advantage in international trade. According to the Pittsburgh Post-Gazette, currency manipulation works when the value of a country's currency is deflated artificially. For example, by buying "massive amounts of foreign currencies," China is able to inflate the value of purchased foreign currencies while deflating the yuan, China's currency. This makes China's products effectively cheaper on the foreign market.[1]

This is not a new tactic for China. As reported by the Wall Street Journal, China has long been manipulating the value of its currency in this way, even going so far as to set a target exchange rate every day between the yuan and the dollar and buying dollars when necessary to keep the value of the yuan artificially deflated.[2]

In a 2015 Wall Street Journal op-ed, Donald
Trump expressed his belief that China's currency
manipulation is responsible for "robbing Americans of
billions of dollars of capital and millions of jobs." China's
currency is undervalued by as much as 40 percent, by some
estimations. By manipulating the yuan, China has created a
"de facto tariff on all imported goods" and moved the
trade balance in its favor. Manipulation of the yuan's value
has not only weakened manufacturing in the United States,
but also the ability of small businesses to compete
internationally and the performance of the agriculture
industry.[3]

Aluminum Dumping

Another unfair business practice China uses is
government subsidies in competitive industries, which
gives Chinese companies an unfair advantage and allows
them to flood the US market with underpriced products.
This practice is known as "dumping," and aluminum is
one of the main metals Chinese companies are dumping in
the U.S. According to the Wall Street Journal, the Obama
administration filed a formal complaint accusing China of
"funneling artificially cheap loans from state-run banks to
Chinese aluminum producers, helping the companies
upgrade their facilities and expand production."[4]

Additionally, in 2010 the Commerce Department
imposed a 374 percent punitive tariff on China's aluminum
imports into the U.S. market because the aluminum
producers were so heavily subsidized by the Chinese
government.[5] The main culprit was China Zhongwang

Holdings Ltd., owned by billionaire businessman Liu
Zhongtian, who was found to be using various methods to
evade punitive tariffs.[6] For example, aluminum was
shipped from China to Mexico to then be sold from
Mexico to Vietnam with the intent of it ultimately being
exported to the U.S.[7]

Steel Dumping by China

"Nearly every military platform and weapon
system in our nation's arsenal is dependent on steel
produced in America," wrote Thomas J. Gibson, president
and CEO of the American Iron and Steel Institute, in the
Pittsburgh Post-Gazette in 2017. Our nation's
infrastructure is heavily reliant on steel. Repeated surges in
internationally subsidized and dumped steel have put the
domestic steel industry at a severe disadvantage. More than
700 million metric tons of excess steel are produced each
year, and more than half of that excess comes from
China.[8] The result is lower steel prices that make it
impossible for American companies to compete. Some
even believe that China is selling its steel at a loss.[9]

In 2018, President Donald Trump imposed a 25
percent tariff on steel imports from most countries in an
effort to level the playing field and revive the United States
steel industry. [10] It remains to be seen whether this policy
will be an effective way to counterbalance China's
practices.

Chinese Rare Earth Metal Ploys

The rare earth industry in China is a huge and
important domestic industry. Rare earth metals are
uncommon metals that must be extracted from ore, and

that have a variety of applications across many industries. They are used to build hybrid vehicles, consumer electronics, high-performance airplanes, and more. While rare earth metals can be found across the globe, according to Wikipedia, "China's reserves are estimated to be 36 million tonnes, or roughly 30 percent of the world's total reserves."[11] To put the rarity of these metals into perspective, a report from the Wall Street Journal noted that, "Whereas annual global copper production is around 15 million tons, most of the rare earth metals produced would comfortably fill a few rail freight wagons. [12]

In 2010 there was a rare earth metal panic when China drastically cut its exports of rare earth metals, hoping to drive prices up. At the time, China produced a staggering 95 percent of the world's marketable rare earth metals. Initially, prices did increase drastically. However, the international market adjusted in a variety of ways, including new mining ventures in countries other than China, better recycling of rare earth metals, and technological research that aimed to decrease the use of rare earth metals in certain products.[13] So in the end, this ploy did not benefit Chinese manufacturers to the extent that they had hoped.

Problems Maintaining Quality

A completely different kind of unfair business practice involves what has been termed "quality fade." Paul Midler's book, *Poorly Made in China*, points out the problem of getting Chinese manufacturers who are creating products for international clients to consistently deliver the quality of product that was agreed upon in the initial contract. Once production is started, the Chinese manufacturer may cut corners by changing the ingredients in the product and even changing the packaging to increase the profit margin. Once the quality slips, it is very difficult for the importer to get the product back to an acceptable quality.[14]

Upcoming Tariff Wars

Recent events may drastically impact some of the practices discussed above. In March 2018, President Trump ordered steep tariffs on almost all steel and aluminum imports into the United States—25 percent on steel and 10 percent on aluminum. Exceptions were granted for Mexico and Canada, and the door was left open to grant exceptions for other U.S. allies in the future.[15] In response, China raised tariffs on 128 U.S. imports, including 25 percent tariffs on pork and scrap aluminum.[16] However, in April 2018 President Trump said he was already considering tariffs on another $100 billion-worth of Chinese goods, and China had already threated to "retaliate forcefully," according to the Wall Street Journal.[17]

This could well become an ongoing "tit-for-tat" that will eventually hurt trade between the U.S. and China, with no one able to predict the extent of the harm in the final outcome.

CHAPTER 17
Chinese Government Censorship
and Repression

Since China is run by the Communist Party
dictatorship, the Chinese government uses its power to
interfere with the free flow of information and news
within the country, unlike democratic countries, where free
press is a hallmark.[1] The Chinese government has
complete control of the press, radio and TV.

This control extends to the internet. Even though
Facebook has over two billion active users worldwide, the
site has been blocked from China.[2] Google and twitter are
similarly unavailable, as are the websites for Time
Mhjagazine, The Economist, Reuters, The Wall Street
Journal, and The New York Times.[3] This ban is imposed
by China's leadership, not the desires of its citizens. A Wall
Street Journal article from 2016 states that Xi Jinping,
China's current leader, has little patience for the influence
of foreign ideas about civil rights and democracy, and
contrasts Xi with his predecessor, Deng Xioaping, who
was more welcoming to foreigners and their ideology.[3]

Sometimes, the Chinese government goes as far as imprisonment to prevent the spread of information. In 2015, a bookseller from Hong Kong who had been involved in selling books banned in mainland China was arrested during a trip to the mainland city of Shenzhen.[4] Although Hong Kong has been part of China since 1997 (it was ruled by the British from 1842-1997), it has a separate capitalist economic system and its own laws and constitution. Therefore, many things that are not legal on the mainland, including the selling of banned books, are still legal in Hong Kong, and mainland authorities have no legal right to punish Hong Kong citizens for these activities. Nonetheless, five booksellers associated with banned book sales in Hong Kong disappeared in 2015, and when one of them, Lam Wing Kee, reappeared in 2016 he said that he had been held in a prison cell and interrogated in the interim.[4]

Beyond its censorship activities, the Chinese government has used many harsh measures to quell dissent and criticism of the government. Dissidents and others have been sent to labor camps, usually without trial, for "reeducation through labor".[5] The sole purpose of this has been to suppress dissent and have all citizens toe the Communist party line. Even Chinese attorneys who represent dissidents get harassed and at times arrested.

It is clear that the Chinese government is unwilling to tolerate the open exchange of ideas that is the foundation of civil rights and a democratic system.

CHAPTER 18
Harvesting Executed Prisoners' Organs in China

Harvesting organs from prisoners is a grisly, inhumane practice that has no place in modern society and medicine. In 2016, an article in Newsweek quoted Ileana Ros-Lehling, then a Congresswoman for the state of Florida, as saying, "China has been perpetuating perhaps some of the most gruesome and egregious human rights violations against the Falun Gong and other prisoners of conscience, yet has hardly faced any criticism, let alone sanctions, for these abuses…The regime's ghoulish and inhumane practice of robbing individuals of their freedom, throwing them in labor camps and prisons, and then executing them and harvesting their organs for transplants is way beyond the pale of comprehension and must be stopped universally and ended unconditionally."[1]

What is the evidence that China engages in
this practice?

1. In 2001, Dr. Wan Guoqi, a doctor from China
who was seeking asylum in the United States, reported that
Chinese government officials were using the organs of
recently-executed prisoners for transplants, even though
the prisoners had not given their consent prior to death.[2]
The Chinese government admits that it did take organs
from prisoners in the past, but says it no longer does so,
and that all organs used for transplants are now voluntarily
donated.[3] However, a number of international
organizations, including Amnesty International and the
United Nations, have continued to investigate these claims.
The practice of harvesting organs from prisoners is
prohibited worldwide by medical ethics standards.

2. There are not enough volunteer organ donors
in China to account for the great number of transplants
carried out. Some Chinese people are culturally opposed to
organ donation. According to a report by BBC.com,
"Many Chinese believe that bodies should remain intact
after death," and this belief therefore acts as a barrier
against organ donation. As of 2014, China had an organ
donation rate of only 0.6 per 1 million people, one of the
world's lowest levels of organ donation.[4] In the same year,
the United States, for instance, had 26 organ donors per
million people, and Spain had the highest rate of organ
donation: 35.3 donors per million.[5] Yet despite this low
rate of donation, a report published in 2016, based on a
10-year study, estimated that 60,000 to 100,000 organ
transplants take place in China every year. The report also

claimed that most of these organs came from prisoners,
and said that the Chinese government's claims that only
10,000 transplants per year were taking place was wildly
inaccurate. The Independent also reported that, "In all,
approximately 1.5 million transplants have been have taken
place at 712 liver and kidney transplant centers across
China since 2000, with over 300,000 of those taking place
at unregulated centers."[6]

3. Not only is the number of transplants done
each year in China quite high, but the waiting time to
receive an organ for transplant is extremely short
compared with the wait in other countries. In Canada, the
average wait time for kidney transplantation is four years.[7]
However, in China patients typically wait a few weeks or
even less for donated organs. Reports find a short wait
time also applies to outsiders who visit the country for
"transplant tourism" and pay top dollar for an organ.[9]
Some investigators believe this is because the organs are
available "on demand," as a prisoner with the desired
organs can be executed whenever an organ is needed.
China carries out more death sentences each year than all
other countries combined.[8] An estimated 2400 people
were executed in China in 2014, according to San
Francisco-based prisoners' rights organization Dui Hua.[9]

Two important books have been written on the
subject of harvesting organs from prisoners in China.
These are *Bloody Harvest: Organ Harvesting of Falun Gong
Practitioners in China*, written by human rights lawyer David
Matas and former Canadian Secretary of State David
Kilgour in 2009, and *The Slaughter: Mass Killings, Organ*

Harvesting, and China's Secret Solution to Its Dissident Problem by
Ethan Gutmann, written in 2014.

According to Matas and Kilgour, members of the
Falun Gong movement are used by the Chinese
government to provide the organs for transplantation.
Falun Gong is a religious/spiritual organization that has
been persecuted by the Chinese government and accused
of being a subversive cult. Falun Gong practitioners in
China are reportedly subjected to a wide range of human
rights abuses, and a 2017 PBS News Hour report
investigated claims from Matas and Gutmann that people
imprisoned for practicing Falun Gong underwent medical
testing to determine whether their organs could be
harvested for transplantation.[10]

Gutmann says that when he interviewed Falun
Gong practitioners who had been jailed and later released,
he began to hear stories about organ harvesting. The detail
that convinced him was the detainees' descriptions of
medical examinations that seemed designed only to test the
condition of their donatable organs, not their overall
health. A 2015 article from The Daily Beast quotes
Gutmann as saying, "A chill went down my spine…I
thought, 'Oh my God, this is a real.'"[11]

Matas' research also found that Chinese hospitals
were charging huge sums for organ transplants: $30,000
for corneal transplants to restore vision, and up to
$130,000 for life-saving transplants of hearts or livers. [11]

Since the Chinese government controls the press
within China, it is unknown whether this practice is still

ongoing. The Chinese do not release information on how many death sentences are carried out in a year. A highly placed Chinese government official, Dr. Huang Jiefu, admitted in 2006 to the practice of harvesting organs from executed prisoners. He is the former deputy health minister for China. Since 2010, Dr. Huang has been working with University of Chicago transplant surgeon Michael Millis to put a new, voluntary system in place and increase regulation of the transplant industry in China, in part by creating an online registry system. Today, he says it has been successful and that illegal transplants are now uncommon in China.[3] But even though there is evidence that this practice is being eliminated, it is very troubling that the practice of harvesting executed prisoners' organs went on for so long and on such a large scale.

REFERENCES

INTRODUCTION
1. John Bryan Starr *Understanding China* Hill and Wong 2010.
2. Foreign Affairs "China Now" May June 2015.
3. Stein Ringen *The Perfect Dictatorship* Hong Kong University Press 2016.
4. Peter Navarro and Greg Autry *Death by China* Pearson Education Inc. 2011.

CHAPTER 1 - DEADLY CARFENTANIL SHIPMENT PROBLEMS FROM CHINA
1. New York Times "Drug maker hid early knowledge of an opioid's abuse" May 29, 2018.
 2. Time.com "Heroin is being laced with a terrifying new substance: what to know about carfentanil" by Josh Sanburn September 12, 2016. Downloaded November 11, 2017.
3. Associated Press via Global News. "Chinese companies willing to export deadly opioid carfentanil to Canada and U.S." October 7, 2016. https://globalnews.ca/news/2989553/chinese-companies-willing-to-export-deadly-opioid-carfentanil-to-canada-and-u-s/
4. National Center for Biotechnology Information. PubChem Compound Database. "Carfentanil." https://pubchem.ncbi.nlm.nih.gov/compound/62156 (accessed Oct. 8, 2018).
5. Apnews.com "China carfentanil ban a 'game-changer' for opioid epidemic." Erika Kinetz, February 16, 2017. Downloaded July 8, 2018.
6. Drug Enforcement Agency. "DEA Issues Carfentanil Warning to Police and Public*" September 22, 2017. Downloaded March 19, 2017*
7. NPR "Lethal Opiate Delivered by Mail from China Killing Addicts in the US". March 11, 2017. Downloaded March 19, 2017.

CHAPTER 2 - TOXIC CHINESE DRYWALL
1. http://www.Merriam-Webster/dictionary/drywall.
2. "An Exciting History of Drywall" by Haniya Rae, The
Atlantic, July 29, 2016.
https://www.theatlantic.com/technology/archive/2016/07/
an-exciting-history-of-drywall/493502/
3. U. S. Government Accountability Office, "Subject:
Information on Defective Drywall." July 31, 2013.
https://www.gao.gov/assets/660/656399.pdf
4. United States Consumer Product Safety Commission.
Downloaded March 14, 2017.
5. Enr.construction.com "ENR:Engineering News
Record/McGraw-Hill Construction" January 28, 2009.
Downloaded March 14, 2017.
6. Remedial Guidance for Homes with Corrosion Problem
Drywall, March 18, 2011. U.S.CPSC and U.S.DHUD.
Downloaded March 14, 2017.
7. Boston Children's Hospital. Pediatric Environmental
Health Center/Health Effects from Chinese Drywall.
Downloaded March 14, 2017.
8. Merlin Law Group, Property Insurance Coverage Law
Blog. Downloaded March 14, 2017.
9. NPRNews.com "Toxic Chinese Drywall Creates a Housing
Disaster" October27, 2009. Downloaded March14, 2017.
10. USAtoday.com "Report Backs Chinese Drywall Health
Complaints" May 2, 2014. Downloaded March 14, 2017.

CHAPTER 3 - TOXIC CHINESE FLOORCOVERING
1. CBSNews.com "Lumber Liquidators" by Anderson
Cooper on 60 Minutes March 1, 2015. Downloaded July 2,
2017.
2. Globalnews.ca "High level of formaldehyde found in
Chinese made floors sold in North America" by Gil Shochat
October 3, 2014. Downloaded July 2, 2017.
3. Consumerreports.org "Breathe easier about your flooring"
by Ed Perratore July 28, 2016.
4. EPA.gov "Questions and answers regarding laminated
flooring" Downloaded July 2, 2017.

5. CNBC.com "Lowes halts sale of Chinese flooring over formaldehyde concerns" by Scott Cohn May 1, 2015.Dowloaded July 2, 2017.
6. CNN.com "Danger of some laminate wood flooring was underestimated report says" by Debra Goldschmidt March 23, 2016. Downloaded July 2, 2017.
7. Forbes.com "60 minutes is right to raise questions about Lumber Liquidators toxic floors" By Elaine Schattner March 2, 2015. Downloaded July 2, 2017.
8. Reuters.com. "Lumber Liquidators settles class-actions related to China-made products." By Reuters Staff. October 24, 2017. Downloaded June 21, 2018.
9. Aboveboardflooring.com "Toxic Chinese laminate flooring" March 3, 2015. Downloaded July 2, 2017.

CHAPTER 4 - TOXIC CHINESE MILK
1. CBSNews.com "Fake milk powder causes baby death" June 9, 2004. Downloaded June 28, 2017.
2. ABC.net.au/news "Fake milk powder kills dozens of Chinese babies: report" April 17, 2004. Downloaded June 28, 2017.
3. Wikipedia.com "Melamine" June 29, 2017.
4. BBC.com "China Dairy Products Found Tainted with Melamine." 9 July 2010.
https://www.bbc.com/news/10565838
5. CSMonitor.com "Behind bad baby milk, an ethical gap in Chinas business" September 17, 2008. Downloaded June 27, 2017.
6. Time.com "Tainted baby milk scandal in China" by Austin Ramzy and Lin Yang September 16, 2008. Downloaded June 27, 2017.
7. Theguardian.com "China executes two for tainted milk scandal" November 24, 2009. Downloaded June 27, 2017.

CHAPTER 5 - TOXIC CHINESE PET FOOD
1. Wikipedia "2007 pet food recalls" Downloaded April 5, 2017.
2. Associated Press. "Tainted pet food a bigger risk to cats than dogs." April 1, 2007. Downloaded July 3, 2018.

3. Barboza, David "Second chemical eyed in Chinese pet food scandal" New York Times. Archived from the original on May 9, 2007. Downloaded on April 5, 2017.
4. News.vin.com "Pet owners receive $12.4 million in melamine case" by Edie Lau October 12, 2011. Downloaded June 26, 2017.
5. USAToday.com " China admits tainted food link" by Calum MacLeod April 26, 2007. Downloaded June 26, 2017.
6. HuffingtonPost.com "Toxic jerky treats responsible for more than 1,000 dog deaths, FDA says" May 19,2014. Downloaded April 11, 2017.
7. NBCNews.com "Jerky Pet Treat Deal: Makers Agree to $6.5 Million Fund" May 30, 2014. Downloaded July 3, 2018.
8. CBSNews.com "Petco pulls pet treats from China suspected of killing, sickening thousands" January 6, 2015. Downloaded April 11, 2017.

CHAPTER 6 - TOXIC CHINESE HEPARIN
1. Wikipedia.com "2008 Chinese heparin adulteration" Downloaded June 28, 3017.
2. NYTimes.com "Heparin contamination may have been deliberate, F.D.A. says" by Gardiner Harris April 30. 2008. Downloaded June 28, 2017.
3. NYTimes.com "Drug Tied to China had Contaminant, F.D.A. says" by Gardiner Harris and Walt Bogdanich March 6, 2008. Downloaded July 5, 2018.
4. FDA.gov "Information on heparin" October 1, 2009. Downloaded June 28, 2017.
5. NYTimes.com "U.S. identifies tainted heparin in 11 countries" by Gardiner Harris April 22, 2008. Downloaded June 28, 2017.

CHAPTER 7 - PROBLEMS WITH CHINESE VACCINES
1. Time.com "China vaccine scandal prompts angry backlash from parents and doctors" by Charlie Campbell March 22, 2016. Downloaded July 4,2017.
2. Rfa.org "Hundreds of Chinese children sickened after out-of-date vaccine: parents" September 21, 2015. Downloaded

July 4, 2017.
3. NYTimes.com "Chinese vaccine scandal threatens public faith in immunizations" by Chris Buckley April 18, 2016. Downloaded July 4, 2017.
4. 6. BBC.com "China vaccine scandal: 37 arrested" March 23, 2016. Downloaded July 4, 2017.
5. Fortune.com "The weak regulators behind China's vaccine scandal" by Scott Cendrowski March 28, 2016. Downloaded July 4, 2017.
6. Time.com "China has begun cracking down on parents protesting substandard vaccines" by Charlie Campbell April 21, 2016. Downloaded July 4, 2017.

CHAPTER 8 - TOXIC TOOTHPASTE AND COUGH SYRUP

1. Nytimes.com "Toxic toothpaste made in China is found in U.S" by Walt Bogdanich June 2, 2007. Downloaded July 5, 2017.
2. Theweek.com "Made in China: seven toxic imports" November 11, 2009. Downloaded July 10, 2017.
3. Reuters.com "Saudi Arabia says finds toxic Chinese toothpaste" August 21, 2007. Downloaded July 10, 2017.
4. Wikipedia.com "2007 Chinese export recalls" Downloaded July 5, 2017.
5. CBC.ca/news "Fake Colgate, Chinese toothpastes pose risks: Health Canada" June 30, 2007. Downloaded July 5, 2017.
6. Scienceblog.com "Some toothpaste from China found to contain toxic chemical" posted by Dr. Charles June 3, 2007. Downloaded July 5, 2017.

CHAPTER 9 - PROBLEMS WITH SOME CHINESE FOODS

1. The week.com "Made in China: seven toxic imports" November 11, 2009. Downloaded July 2017.
2. Eltecolte.org "Be careful of what candy you eat, too many have lead as toxic as sweet" BuXahej Bajpur October 26, 2012. Downloaded July 18, 2017.

3. Naturenews.com "Halloween warning: candy made in China may be contaminated with melamine" by Mike Adams October 31, 2008. Downloaded July 17, 2017.
4. Economist.com "The most neglected threat to public health in China is toxic soil" June 8, 2017. Downloaded July 19, 2017.
5. Theepochtimes.com "Chinas toxic rice problem" by Michelle Yu March 3, 2011. Downloaded July 19, 2017.
6. Theweeks.com "Made in China: seven toxic imports" November 11, 2009. Downloaded July 10, 2017.
7. Chinadaily.com "Tainted ginger a health hazard" May 9 2012. Downloaded July 10, 2017.
8. Foodsafetynews.com "Asian honey, banned in Europe, is flooding U.S. grocery shelves" by Andrew Schneider August 15, 2011. Downloaded July 24, 2017.
9. Time.com "Tainted Chinese honey may be on U.S. store shelves" by Meredith Melnick August 22, 2011. Downloaded July 24, 2017.
10. Nbcnews.com "Chinese eggs tainted by excessive melamine" October 26, 2008. Downloaded July 27, 2017.
11. Nyttimes.com "Melamine is discovered in more eggs from China" by Andrew Martin October 29, 2008. Downloaded July 27, 2017.
12. Time.com "Bad eggs: another food scandal rocks China" by Patrick Boehler November 6, 2012. Downloaded July 25, 2017.
13. Hoaxorfact.com "Chinas fake eggs made of plastic- fact analysis" by Siddhartha. Downloaded July 25, 2017.
14. Scmp.com "Preserved egg companies shut in toxic chemical scandal" June 16, 2013. Downloaded July 25, 2017.
15. Wikipedia.com "Gutter oil" Downloaded July 25, 2017.
16. Washingtonpost.com "You may never again eat street food in China again after watching this video" by Max Fisher October 28, 2013. Downloaded July 26, 2017.
17. Theguardian.com "Vinegar contaminated with antifreeze kills Chinese muslims at Ramadan meal" buy Associated Press August 22, 2011. Downloaded August 4, 2017.
18. Cbsnews.com "Chemical infused watermelons explode in

China" May 17, 2011. Downloaded August 2, 2017.
19. Theepochtimes.com "More tainted buns found in China"
April 19, 2011. Downloaded August 2, 2017.
20. Telegraph.co.uk "Top ten Chinese food scandals" by
peter Foster April 27, 2011. Downloaded August 2,2017.
21. Shangaiexpat.com "Ten dumpling stores shut down for
selling aluminum infused Baozi" September 26,
2016.Downloaded August 4, 2017.
22. Epicurious.com "Why Aluminum-free Baking Powder is
Better." by David Tamarkin.
https://www.epicurious.com/ingredients/why-aluminum-
free-baking-powder-is-better-article. August 11, 2015.

CHAPTER 10 - PROBLEMS WITH CHINESE MEAT AND SEAFOOD

1. Seattletimes.com "China regulators fine OSI Group $3.6
million in 2014 meat scandal." By Kelvin Chan. October 3,
2016. https://www.seattletimes.com/business/china-
regulators-fine-osi-group-3-6m-in-2014-meat-scandal/
2. Time.com "China: tainted pork renews food safety fears"
By Jessie Jiang March 23, 2011. Downloaded August 2, 2017.
3. Newyorktimes.com "Rat meat sold as lamb highlights fear
in China" By Chris Buckley May 3, 2013. Downloaded
August 8 2017.
4. Newyorktimes.com "Food safety in China faces big
hurdles" By Michael Moss and Neil Gough July 24, 2014.
5. Theguardian.com "Can China Kick Its Animal Antibiotic
Habit?" By Charlotte Middlehurst. June 19, 2018.
https://www.theguardian.com/environment/2018/jun/19/c
an-china-kick-its-animal-antibiotic-habit.
6. Foodsafetynews.com "China's food safety issues worse
than you thought" By Nancy Huehnergarth July 11, 2014.
Downloaded July 29, 2017.
7. Telegraph.co.uk "Top 10 Chinese food scandals" By Peter
Foster April27, 2011. Downloaded August 2, 2017.
8. Nytimes.com "Anything goes in China's food system" July
25, 2014.
9. Newyorktimes.com "Rat meat sold as lamb highlights fear

in China" by Chris Buckley May 3, 2013. Downloaded August 8, 2017.

10. TheAtlantic.com "Walmart China accidentally sold fox meat to people who really wanted donkey meat" By Alexander Arad-Santos January 2014, Downloaded August 8, 2017.

11. Fishwatch.gov. "The Global Picture - Global Aquaculture Production." https://www.fishwatch.gov/sustainable-seafood/the-global-picture. Downloaded August 28, 2018.

12. Newyorktimes.com "F.D.A. issues alert on Chinese seafood" by Andrew Martin June 29, 2007, Downloaded August 2, 2017.

13. Washingtonpost.com "FDA halts imports of some Chinese seafood" by Frank Ahrens June 29, 2007. Downloaded August 2, 2017.

14. ABCnews.go.com "FDA halts imports of farmed fish from China" by Steven Renberg June 28, 2007. Downloaded August 2, 2017.

15. TheLancet.com "Food supply and safety issues in China" June 8, 2013. Downloaded July 19, 2017. https://www.thelancet.com/journals/lancet/article/PIIS014 0-6736(13)60776-X/fulltext

CHAPTER 11 - TOXIC CLOTHING FROM CHINA

1. Fowler JF Jr., Skinner SM, Belsito DV. "Allergic contact dermatitis from formaldehyde resins in permanent press clothing: an underdiagnosed cause of generalized dermatitis" Journal of the American Academy of Dermatology. December 1992, 962-8. https://www.ncbi.nlm.nih.gov/pubmed/1479102

2. De Groot AC et al. "Formaldehyde-releasers: relationship to formaldehyde contact allergy. Part 2," Contact Dermatitis. 2010 July ;63(1):1-9. https://www.ncbi.nlm.nih.gov/pubmed/20236157

3. Alternative-za-vas.com "Are we poisoning ourselves with our clothes?" by Ozren Podnar. Downloaded August 19, 2017.

4. United States Accountability Office. Report to

Congressional Committee" Formaldehyde in Textiles"
August 2010 GAO-10-875. Downloaded August 18, 2017.
5. Nytimes.com "When wrinkle free clothing also means
formaldehyde fumes."December 11, 2010, Downloaded
August 18, 2017.

CHAPTER 12 - TOXIC CHINESE TOYS

1. Poisonedpets.com "50% of toys from China contain toxins
, study reveals" Downloaded July 11, 2017.
2. Telegraph.co.uk.com "One third of Chinese toys contain
heavy metals" by Malcolm Moore and James Hall December
8, 2011. Downloaded July 11, 2017.
3. Forbes.com "The most toxic toys" December 16, 2008.
Downloaded August 6, 2017.
4. Thestreet.com "China has a history of selling dangerous
products to U.S. consumers" by Emily Stewart March 3,
2015. Downloaded August 30, 2017.
5. Telegraph.co.uk.com "One third of Chinese toys contain
heavy metals" by Malcolm Moore and James Hall December
8, 2011. Downloaded July 11, 2017.
6. Parentmap.com "Toxic toys: tips for choosing safe toys for
kids" by Maria Bellos Fiaher February 24, 2012. Downloaded
August 26, 2017.
7. Nydailynews.com "Toxic lead replaced by even more toxic
cadmium in children's toys, trinkets" by Nicole Lyn Pesce
January 11, 2010. Downloaded September 2, 2017.
8. Wikipedia.com "2007 Chinese export recalls" Downloaded
July 5, 2017.

CHAPTER 13 - CHINESE HACKING AND INDUSTRIAL ESPIONAGE

1. Pittsburgh Post-Gazette from New York Times "N. Korea
bid to breach banks discovered" by Paul Mazur and Choe
Sang-Hun March 26, 2017.
2. Wikipedia.com "Cyberwarfare in China" downloaded
March 2017.
3. Pittsburgh Post-Gazette "Five Chinese officials indicted
for hacking" by Rich Lord and Tracie Mauriello May 20,

2014.

4. MIT Technology Review. "Cyber-Espionage Nightmare."
David Talbot. June 10, 2015. Accessed July 23, 2018.
https://www.technologyreview.com/s/538201/cyber-
espionage-nightmare/

5. Renewableenergy.com "60 minutes investigates Chinese
cyberespionage in wind mill industry" January 18, 2016.

6. Npr.org "It was a company with a lot of promise. Then a
Chinese customer stole its technology."
https://www.npr.org/2018/04/09/599557634/it-was-a-
company-with-a-lot-of-promise-then-a-chinese-customer-
stole-its-technol. April 9, 2018.

7. Reuters.com "China's Sinovel Convicted in US of Trade-
secret Theft." https://www.reuters.com/article/us-sinovel-
wind-gro-usa-court/chinas-sinovel-convicted-in-u-s-of-trade-
secret-theft-idUSKBN1FD2XL January 24, 2018.

8. Financial Times "German fears of China cyber spying
reinforced by US charges."
https://www.ft.com/content/a673bcf2-e0f7-11e3-a934-
00144feabdc0 by Jeevan Vasagar and Chris Bryant May 21,
2014.

9. New York Times. "Chinese Hackers Pursue Key Data on
US Workers."
https://www.nytimes.com/2014/07/10/world/asia/chinese-
hackers-pursue-key-data-on-us-workers.html?_r=0. July 9,
2014.

10. Dailymail.com "Chinese J20 stealth jet based on military
plans 'stolen' by hackers makes debut" by Ryan O'Hare
November 1, 2016.

CHAPTER 14 - CHINESE HACKING OF THE
NUCLEAR AND SOLAR ENERGY SECTOR

1. Pittsburgh Post-Gazette "Westinghouse data stolen
despite big deal with China" by Anya Litvak May 20, 2014.

2. Time.com "Here's what Chinese hackers actually stole
from U.S. companies" by Sam Frizell May 20, 2014.

3. Pittsburgh Post-Gazette "Engineer pleads guilty in illegal
aid" January 9, 2017.

4. Powersource.post-gazette.com "Nuclear secrets: the ex-Westinghouse employee accused of helping a foreign power" September 15, 2016.
5. Time.com "Here's what Chinese hackers actually stole from U.S. companies" by Sam Frizell May 20, 2014. Downloaded September 27, 2017.
6. New York Times "Solar industry is rebalanced by U.S. pressure on China" by Diane Cardwell and Keith Bradsher July 26, 2014.

CHAPTER 15 - CHINESE COUNTERFEITING OF CDs AND DVDs

1. Techcrunch.com "Chinese pirates account for 92% of counterfeit CDs and DVDs in EU" by Peter Ha June 1,2007. Downloaded September 30, 2017.
2. Factsanddetails.com "Pirating and counterfeiting in China" by Jeffrey Hays 2008 updated March 2012. Downloaded September 30, 2017.
3. Youtube.com "China destroys 16 million counterfeit CDs and DVDs" July 21, 2015. Downloaded September 30, 2017.
4. Upi.com "China launches CD/DVD anti-piracy campaign" by Christian Wade August 13, 2002. Downloaded September 30, 2017.

CHAPTER 16 - CHINA'S UNFAIR BUSINESS PRACTICES

1. Pittsburgh Post-Gazette "Heard Off the Street: Advocates call out China on currency" by Len Boselovic March 1, 2014.
2. Wall Street Journal "Currency manipulation is a real problem" by Judy Shelton February 13, 2017.
3. Wall Street Journal "Ending China's currency manipulation" by Donald J. Trump November 9, 2015.
4. Wall Street Journal "U.S. targets China in metals fight" by Scott Patterson and William Mauldin January 12, 2017.
5. Wall Street Journal "U.S. Seizes $25 Million Worth of Aluminum Linked to Chinese Billionaire" January 13, 2017.
6. Wall Street Journal "U.S. Says Aluminum Exports From Chinese Firm Evaded Restrictions" November 8, 2016.

7. Wall Street Journal "Money From Chinese State Giants
Helped Fund Aluminum Stockpile." May 11, 2017.
8. Pittsburgh Post-Gazette "Steel: an industry under attack"
by Thomas J. Gibson September 18, 2017.
9. Durham University "Factcheck: is China dumping steel?"
by Ian Greenwood and Ray Hudson June 15, 2017.
10. CNBC.com "Trump Says his Tariffs are Saving the US
Steel Industry." https://www.cnbc.com/2018/08/16/trump-
says-his-tariffs-are-saving-us-steel-industry.html August 16,
2018.
11. Wikipedia "Rare earth industry in China" downloaded
September 29, 2017.
12. Wall Street Journal "Notable and quotable: rare earth
economics " February 4, 2016.
13. Wall Street Journal "China's rare-earth bust" July 20,2016.
14. Paul Midler "Poorly Made in China" John Wiley & Sons
Inc. 2011.
15. NPR.org "Trump Formally Orders Tariffs on Steel,
Aluminum Imports" by Scott Horsley March 8, 2018.
16. Global Policy Watch "China Raises Tariffs on 128 U.S.
Imports in Retaliation for U.S. Section 232 Steel and
Aluminum Tariffs" by Ashwin Kaja, Christopher Adams and
Gina M. Vetere April 3, 2018.
17. Wall Street Journal "China Set to Counter Tariffs." By
Lingling Wei April 7-8, 2018.

CHAPTER 17 - CHINESE GOVERNMENT
CENSORSHIP AND REPRESSION
1. Stein Ringen "The Perfect Dictatorship" published by
Hong Kong University Press 2016.
2. Wall Street Journal "Facebook's big China comeback is
stalling" by Alyssa Abkowitz, Deepa Seetharaman and Eva
Dou January 31, 2017.
3. Wall Street Journal "Looking to Mao, Beijing pulls
welcome mat for foreigners" by Andrew Browne May 4,2016.
4. Wall Street Journal "Bookseller describes detention in
China" by Isabella Steger June 17, 2016.

5. Wall Street Journal "Chinese think tank criticizes labor camps as outdated" by Brian Spegele August 8, 2013.

CHAPTER 18 - HARVESTING EXECUTED
PRISONERS' ORGANS IN CHINA
1. Newsweek.com "Is China still harvesting organs from its political prisoners? " June 15, 2016. Downloaded April 3, 2017;
2. CNN.com "Kill and Cull: China Rejects Doctor's Testimony."
http://www.cnn.com/2001/WORLD/asiapcf/east/06/28/c hina.organ/
3. The Washington Post. "China used to harvest organs from prisoners. Under pressure, that practice is finally ending." By Simon Denyer. September 15, 2017.
https://www.washingtonpost.com/world/asia_pacific/in-the-face-of-criticism-china-has-been-cleaning-up-its-organ-transplant-industry/2017/09/14/d689444e-e1a2-11e6-a419-eefe8eff0835_story.html?utm_term=.ecb2069b8cfb
4. BBC News "China to stop harvesting prisoners organs" Downloaded April 3, 2017.
5. PBS.org "Which country has the highest organ donation rates?" May 10, 2014.
https://www.pbs.org/newshour/health/country-highest-organ-donation-rates
6. The Independent "China carrying out over 60,000 illegal organ transplants annually, report finds" June 29 2016. Downloaded April 3,2017.
7. CBC.ca. "Toronto man's wait for kidney transplant highlights shortage of donors." March 29, 2018.
https://www.cbc.ca/news/canada/toronto/toronto-transplant-kidney-search-1.4599155
8. The Washington Post. "China's Capital Cases Still Secret, Arbitrary." By Maureen Fan and Ariana Eunjung Cha. December 24, 2008.
9. Newsweek. "China Executed 2,400 Prisoners Last Year Says a Human Rights Group." By Madeline Grant. October 21, 2014. https://www.newsweek.com/china-executed-2400-

prisoners-2013-says-human-rights-group-278733
10. PBS.org "Has China really stopped obtaining organs from executed prisoners?"
https://www.pbs.org/newshour/show/china-still-gathering-organs-executed-prisoners
11. The Daily Beast "Does China harvest organs from living prisoners?" September 29, 2015. Downloaded April 3, 2017.

ABOUT THE AUTHOR

Andrejs Baumhammers was born in Riga, Latvia on October 12, 1935. His family lived in the independent republic of Latvia. In 1940, Latvia was occupied by the communist USSR, followed by Nazi occupation from 1941-1944, when the Soviets returned. His family left Latvia for Germany in 1944, to escape having to live under Soviet communist occupation again. From 1945 to 1950 the Baumhammers lived in the DP (Displaced Person) camps of Fishbach and Wurtzburg. In 1950 his family emigrated to Pittsburgh, Pennsylvania where he pursued his education at the University of Pittsburgh, earning B.S. and D.D.S. degrees in 1959. Upon graduation he also married fellow Latvian and dentist (1962) Inese Dzintars. He served four years in the US Army Dental Corps and in 1965 completed his training in Periodontics at Eastman Dental Center and University of Rochester with a M.S. degree. He has been a full time (1967-1974) and then part-time faculty member of the School of Dental Medicine of University of Pittsburgh from 1967 until now (2019). Because of the stress and trauma of WWII he developed a keen interest in international affairs, which led him to pursue writing this book. He is a staunch anti-communist and has a strong antipathy against fascists and dictators.

www.ingramcontent.com/pod-product-compliance
Lightning Source LLC
Chambersburg PA
CBHW070317240526
45467CB00045B/531